gusher

"Christopher Soden's poems are never a PR campaign for the author, never self-aggrandizing below a thin veil of manufactured vulnerability. These are not poems created to incite sighs from the audience. They are much more real than that, much more truly vulnerable than that, much more sticky and fun and difficult than that. Often life is solitary, often life is a mother-fucker, but if you are holding this book in your hands then you are not alone, even more than that: you are being held in the arms of an author who may not know you but, in each and every poem, wonders and cares about you."

— **Matthew Dickman author of *Wonderland***

"Honesty and vulnerability abound in this collection of Whitman-like raptures. Christopher Stephen Soden doesn't just tell us that "There are all kinds of attachment /and all kinds of men"; he takes us on a tour through the erotics of male companionship and unabashed desire. Youth, lover, and sage present themselves to the reader in turn, each inviting the reader to engage in a "pas de deux /with...poppa spirit, Animus.""

—**Michael McKeown Bondhus author of *Divining Bones***

Christopher Soden is a poet of being and becoming, of rising above guilt, shame, abuse and humiliation to build a life of love and self-acceptance. Inside the word revision lies, of course, the word *vision*. Gusher, a redux of Christopher Soden's brilliant first book Closer, offers the reader insight into the vision and visionary scope and spirit of this poet. The poems in this collection show us how desire, loss, and nostalgia can come alive inside language, remembering hunger, and hungering for memory. Poem after poem takes your breath away and in doing so reminds you that you're still breathing

—**sam sax, Author of *Madness***

Learning to be oneself and to love oneself is the central narrative in Gusher, a remarkable book about a gay man growing up in Dallas, Texas in the 1980s.

Poetry begins in wonder which leads to desire which completes itself in song. Christopher Soden's poems, often based on a memory of his adolescent sexual awakening, explore the wonder of accepting and realizing his desires. A boy growing up in Dallas, Texas is faced with many challenges, especially if he's gay. In that culture (which is my culture as well as Soden's) boys are routinely abused. Soden writes of his neighbor Jimmy "whose father made him/ strip before hitting him." And his friend Ronnie whose alcoholic mother alternated between stropping him and seducing him. The narrator recalls the horrifying relationship he engaged in with an older boy:

> the cold
> dread in your gut when Trev showed up
> ringing your doorbell, over and over,
> determined to deliver the beating
> you always knew was coming

To protect his sanity in this perverse and hostile culture, the speaker desperately imagines himself a perpetual outsider, a stranger from a far kingdom:

> I would not presume to instruct
> you on the care of outcasts,
> only suggest a country's values
> are reflected in the treatment
> of its prisoners. You cannot imagine
> how I miss my home.
> > *My kingdom is far away*

Inhabiting this kingdom of the imagination allows the boy to create a world where love is possible. Inspired by his cinematic mentor James Dean, the speaker aspires toward 'exquisite expression of undistilled/ Dionysian celebration' and he learns to

> ...take your life
> into your own hands, even if it lasts
> only a few moments
> > *The World in a Book of Matches*

And in this way, the boy discovers the beauty of desire:

> dance the dance that had
> always beckoned, aloft finally in the pas de deux
> with my poppa-spirit, Animus.
> > *Jockstrap*

> scrub me
> from heel to nape from wattle to taint and behind
> my ruddy scruffy jug ears buff me till i squeak
> fit me with harness brushed new feathers ready
> to taunt the sun
> > *buddy scrub*

Christopher Soden is a poet of being and becoming, of rising above guilt, shame, abuse and humiliation to build a life of love and self-acceptance.

> **— Michael Simms, Author of *American Ash***

gusher

poems by
Christopher Stephen Soden

QUEERMOJO
A Rebel Satori Imprint
New Orleans

Published in the United States of America by
Rebel Satori Press
www.rebelsatoripress.com

Poems included in *Gusher* also appeared in: *Ganymede Poets: One, ArliJo, Off the Rocks, Assaracus, Texas Observer, The James White Review, Illya's Honey, Collective Brightness, Polari Jornal, Velvet Mafia, Poetry Super Highway, Gents, Bad Boys and Barbarians, Windy City Times, Best Texas Writing 2.*

Paperback ISBN: 978-1-60864-233-5
ebook ISBN: 978-1-60864-234-2

Gusher is dedicated to my sisters, Victoria and Penelope, my nephew, Daniel, my dear friends, Ann Howells, Frederick Mensch, Joan Larkin, Paul Koniecki, Lisa Huffaker, Robin Turner, Sion Pryor, Ben Schroth, Jason Edwards, Matthew Dickman, Michael Simms, and Betty, my fierce, remarkable, funny, brilliant mother, who looked out for me, took care of me, protected me, and never cared that I was queer.

Thank you, sweet friends, for your warmth, encouragement, care and love.

Contents

Closer redux: an introduction

Some time during the latter part of 2010 and its release in June 2011, *Closer* was a source of worry for me. Some serious health issues had arisen, and irrational or not, I was afraid that my demise might be imminent. I say this in all candor, as a man whose life has not been especially marked by careful, deliberate reasoning. Whether or not my bipolar disorder or anxiety or depression, et al was the culprit, who can say? I can only tell you I did not wish to pass over, without a single collection of poetry to my name. Knowing that contemporary tropes required a tight collection of poems that followed a thematic thread and narrative arc, I opted instead for the sort of "best of" assortment that was premature. I gathered my strongest poems, and even after cutting those by half, still wound up with a text of 99 pages. Another taboo. Too long for a single book of poetry. At least by any serious standard of evaluation. The resulting book was met with more than a little gracious critical response. But my knowledge that it wasn't as strong; as focused and purposeful as it might have been, nagged at me. Understand, I am proud of *Closer*, but couldn't shake the feeling that I'd neglected my obligation as an author to be meticulous and always aim high.

When I approached Sven Davisson, my editor at **Rebel Satori/ QueerMojo**, with the idea of a revised edition, he was good with it. He also mentioned that it was the 10th Anniversary of *Closer*, and therefore, fortuitous. I engaged the help of Brian Clements and Cindy Huyser to edit the revised edition. After years of working with the manuscript myself, and acquaintance with the material, I'd reached a saturation point. I felt it only smart to engage the wisdom of other eyes and ears.

They put in considerable time and evaluation, assessing the best poems to keep, the most effective running order, and those which felt extraneous to salient content.

As I processed the particulars of this project, it occurred to me that by considering *Closer* in a new light, the revised collection might arguably comprise an altogether different book; that tells a story, if you will. The strategy used by Clements and Huyser was to create a narrative, as opposed to cherry picking for the sake of variety and opulence. I struggled with whether or not this explanation was necessary, or if it gave this re-imagined and re-conceived assortment short-shrift. After much agonizing, I concluded that for the sake of transparency, I should own this decision. And change the title. I was pleased with the quality of *Closer* but these particular poems, seemed to beg for a more cohesive and cogent orchestration. Here, then, is *Gusher.*

Gusher

1

The world in a book of matches

This is the start of your life,
and the end. Nothing is just
as it appears, though you have come
to understand that face value, the apparent
world, amounts to everything.
You are waiting for your taxi, a storm
fermenting in the cluster of black clouds
to the north. You reach into the pocket
of a white dinner jacket, you haven't worn
since the previous Spring, and find yourself
holding a red book of forgotten matches.
They are a clue to your lost dreams.
There is a name written jauntily
on the front. The name of a club.
Cicero's. Some corny joint
a friend from out of town dragged
you to. Yeah. Now it's coming back.
Where the waiters wear souvenir ties
from Des Moines and ear studs.
The singer is an androgynous albino
with a crew cut, who knows the words
to *Skylark* in bad French. You despise
these bohemian dives in the arts district.
You never believed you deserved
the scrumptious boy across the table,
enjoying a shot of good bourbon
with you, and smiling
without pretense. And eventually

7

he will come to agree.
But on this one cool evening
in early Spring, he lets you
light his Winston, invites you
to join him while he visits
the Men's Room. In the way
men sometimes will. His question
makes your ears tingle.
He cannot ask you to dance
because the book of matches
was painted and printed and folded
and cut and stapled by guys
in a factory, in a town, in a state,
in a country, in a nation,
on a water planet, in a galaxy,
in the universe, in the reckoning
of God. Where they don't strike
that sort of flame, and it's not
that kind of club. But none
of this matters. Because
when you have the boy
and the bourbon, and the Winstons
and the music and the question,
and when you say,
yes, oh yes Then you take
your life in your own hands,
even if it lasts only
a few moments.

Gusher

James Dean stepped up and stepped
out early in his voluptuously tragic
career, proclaiming bi-sexual
inclinations to the press in the 1950's:
*Why go through life with one hand
tied behind your back?* And even if
you never heard that now
notorious quote, it didn't take Freud
to decode the tenderness he showed
Plato in *Rebel Without a Cause*
or dangerous need he shared
on the ferris wheel with Abra
in *East of Eden*. Pissed
and despondent. Defiant fringe-dweller
who ached for other men
and women with ferocity,
equally prone to romance, or havoc.
It wasn't until filming *Giant*,
though, that he realized
the exquisite expression of undistilled
Dionysian celebration. Irresistible
poison of degeneracy. As Jett Rink,
ranch-hand at *The Reata*, buttoning
sheepskin coat against the merciless
cold of west Texas, he measures his
plot, walking boot heel to toe, rigging
a primitive wooden tower
to house his insistent, chugging

9

drill. He keeps vigil to
this scrap wood contraption
as if a priest in a stone temple.
Eventually, something roiling
beneath layers of rock and fossil, clay
and loam reaches the shaft of his
derrick and he climbs, hoisting
himself up and up till he reaches
the crest of that miraculous
conduit, black syrup dense and pitchy
as liquid night. Dean welcomes this
infernal downpour of bliss, stretching
his arms to receive a baptism
of careless, criminal love.

Outcast

When I watch television documentaries
about sociopaths, kept in basements
with mildewed mattresses and converted
appliances I think, "How could you save them?
How could they help themselves after that?"

But it all collapses when I remember
Jimmy. Even though his father made him
strip before beating him. Even though
his folks were kids themselves when he

came along. Jimmy lived next door
and invited me but I never
considered it. Most boys didn't
get me anyway, and he'd take swipes
at my manhood. It's easy
to love a criminal when you see

James Dean or Matt Dillon
or River Phoenix with a smoke
and cool jacket. Misunderstood.
Too ignorant not to say
what everyone's thinking.
Swinging furiously between the poles
of *dont you like me* and *fuck off.*

But gorgeous, reddish-blonde Jimmy,
grubby and arrogant, wanted you

to follow him to the woods. Do something
unforgettable and ugly. Like he knew
you wanted that. He befriended a dowager

hermit in a frail wooden mansion. Surrounded
by tomcat familiars, she brewed Hibiscus
tea and taught him the violin. We laughed
when the paper said he'd lost his only
consort in a fire. Too easy

to imagine him punishing her
because she was cross, or had enough
or failed some test. I was 13
when I passed on a family
reunion to stay home and spend

the afternoon at the movies.
When I came back to swarms
of cops and fire engines,
the conical black and green trees
ignited behind my house. How
the sparks fluttered and spun
in the grimy winter wind.

My kingdom is far away

And though I cannot hear
the notes of my songbird,
or glimpse his plumage,
I will not forget the sanctity

of my birth. I do not
expect to be honored
here, though the God
who harvested your stars
plucked mine as well.

Forgive me if I think
some of your subjects slow,
my passions confound them
somehow, repulse them,
as if they found a child
raiding the sugar bowl.

As if they cannot
understand that sweet
is sweet. If you could
only smell the dark
blossoms of my country.
Taste the fruits
of our orchards,

I would name them
for you, weave them

into the great tent
of our history. It is
always easy to mock
another's customs, paths
that terrify or astonish.

While I am supposed to believe
that casting salt or imbibing
ersatz blood or the cloaking
of brides are the practices
of an enlightened culture.

I would not presume
to instruct you
on the care of outcasts.
Only suggest a country's values
are reflected in the treatment
of its prisoners. You cannot imagine

how I miss my home.
My groom. Even now
he is filling the basin
with hot water
and lather. He is daubing
his temples with a rich,
delectable salve.

He is singing
my name, to the weary
sun. He is asking
the sovereign

of all worlds
for my safe return.

2

Drive-in movie

I like your baby blue convertible,
luster and dazzle of chrome
flanks and jewelry, combustible
chariot of locomotion, cloud chaser
you navigate to collect me. I climb
aboard, drown in stereo bop
and cool cool yes yes careening
from jazz riffs and licks, while
rough wind teases and buffets
our hair. Doesn't matter
what's playing tonight
cause it's enough
just having you
this close. Behind the screen the canvas
is seven stories high. Makes me
think of days before I was
an itch, when my folks came here.
Egg-paint picture of circus with clowns
and ponies and tigers and acrobats.
Acrobats can dive fearlessly
and land on their feet just so.
The sun is sinking as we pay and hook
the speaker to your door.
Watermelon pink evening sky suffuses
and darkens: now cranberry, raspberry,
dewberry, huckleberry, plum.
Trailer music kicks in: *kiss kiss bang bang.*
Night air warm and plausible

flows like tides of blood pounding
and ticking. Tainting our skin.
I've got vodka mixed with crushed
lemon and sugar and ice and cut
strong peel into strips. It goes down
really nice. Your scent steeps
and billows, coats my neck and
arms. "Baby, what are we
gonna do? Will we make it
out alive? Wait wait wait wait wait.
Lemme think." Chuckles bubble
between us slow and languid.
Mosquitoes probe and tap my arms
as I tap you. Your mouth
sour, smoky, scalding. The stars
and crickets, they turn,
they turn away.

Cowboys

What do you suppose
it is about men, when we are
small, our folks dress us
to be cowboys. Chaps,

pointed-toe boots, fringe, holsters,
hammer cap pistols, tethered
felt ten-gallon hats, shirts with snap
fastened mother-of-pearl buttons.

I believe we wanted it too.
Our horses, Castor and Pollux,
would drag us headlong
into swoon of velocity,
rollicking oceans
of prairie grass our dominion.

Tamarind and copperhead,
grouse and javelina,
stone and iguana
submerged in the vortex
of our flight. Lives would be

taken judiciously. Rustlers,
horse thieves, cardsharps.
We would learn to recognize
by blanket, paint and bracelet,
Indians we could trust. You and I

take turns crooning
the cattle to sleep, swap dreams
by red and purple watchfire.
After supper, snore together,
arms tangled in a careless net

of reassurance. Under vast
milk splash of throbbing stars.
In the morning lather
the other's back, if we could
find a spangly brook.

When I was a boy cowboy
I didn't know you
were waiting. Didn't know
what Great Father Spirit
had in mind. The surprises

I would give the man
and woman whose longing
or boredom set my clock.
Didn't know what my willy was
for. Couldn't hardly look down.

I have heard all men
want to be cowboys,
something pulls them
westward to that golden plain

of living. Being what's happening
right now. What did Father Spirit

uncover when he tore back
an empty sky over the world
for buckaroos? Just us boys
together?

the hand i was dealt

i knew you in halls and tawdry yellow
gloss of first school days ashen sky
of recess before i understood words
like *queer sissy faggot* from bruisers
too cool for smarts while i failed
to comprehend the history of that
transaction: fathers conferring failure
upon sons and sons transmitting
futility to other sons of living
up to repugnance of their dicks
or thinking another boy
had anything to offer you hand
withdrawn the other lad forever
backing away smiling you spat
hubris and contempt before i
realized id made some mistake
you might say the clock
and personal witness have only
vindicated me though how
to explain your clammy paw
priming my languid manhood
under gods cold mercury
vapor angels in parking lot
of cruise park i could not
begin to say

Jockstrap

When I was a kid, maybe, thirteen,
maybe younger, I was a towel boy
at a men's health club, not far from brimming,
blue, Jewel Lake. A sweeping, melodic
hum drifted from that valley, to my ears,
a sweet, cold achy sound that pricked
the tympanic hymen, buried deep
in those caverns. The guys would come

from running or weight lifting or tennis or a swim
and start to undress, spreading arms, arching
backs, stretching or touching or jostling
with ease and comfort of those
who are naked and celebrating
company of those like themselves.

Naked together, wearing clothes
or not. It's all the same. We share
radio equipment. Radio. Radio.
I'm the same with you. The music
of raucous play a symphony
of light, as if sun, moon, stars, comets,
had broken and drenched me
in liquid blaze. These angels

I heard as I climbed the summit
of virility. There was one guy
who caught me. Arms strong and brown

as caramel, with kind, feral
eyes. Smile unfolding flower
from another galaxy, exquisite
and tantalizing. Down to his jockstrap,

he walked over, winking. *Help me out,
here, chief, I'm sopping.* I choke
on my heartbeat. His thighs and ass
creamy marble, wet glossy black hair
matted just outside the cleft. I know
the towels are here, and look,
under the counter, the cabinets

behind and to the left. Finally
he points to them. Stacked
in the corner, behind the stool. I blush.
There's an expression
on his face when I hand him
the fluffy, warm towel.
I was the only one who could
help him. Cold grief
washes through my chest.

He hops onto another guy's back,
(loping the locker room)
who snaps his jock, gasping,
laughing breathlessly. He shucks
the strap and disappears
into the shower. Peter balls dangling
black grapes. I hear his heroic singing
over the water. Wagner or Grieg.

A frantic moxie seizes and I grab
the sling hanging from his locker door,
still damp with his sweat, frothy
with salt musk, breath from the ocean,
bandage only men wear,
or need. Cradle for cock and sac,
from the world of men, I saw

my man-buddy peel. I hear him
bellowing thunderclouds and courage
and mountains and fjords, and nick
the jock like Prometheus stealing fire
from heaven, stuffing it
in my sweat pants.

After the sun has gone low, swallowed
all the radiance he spilt before,
and moon commenced her chilly sulk.
I sneak home with my marvel harness,
pulling it over my own downy
willy, blossoming to fill. Turn in

the mirror to see waistband marking
divide between the small of my back
and skinny ass. How my nates poke.
I feel the rush of dominion and buoyant
joy splashing heart chambers, toy body

suddenly a host, a channel, a tissue
too trembly and fragile to contain this
gushing recklessness. A nectarine

swollen with juice. I climb out
and yanking it over my head, drowning,
in dark reek of maleness and changing

rooms, brothels, urinal troughs, smokers, flop houses,
strip joints, prisons, hunting cabins, peep shows,
bath houses, bus terminals, railway cars, barracks,
orphan beds, dancing the dance that always
beckoned, aloft finally in pas de deux
with poppa-spirit, *Animus.*

buddy scrub

there was something about the guys
at summer camp when i was fifteen
who were my friend even ones
i didn't know who smiled
and talked to me as we shucked
glad to shed sticky grimy pungent
layers of duds greasy grassy juicy
tees to dribbled in and skiddy bvds
crusty sock and briny jock dropping
and piling music of impromptu song
mixing with whistle and fart and guffaw
as first blast ice bath roiling geyser hit
sopping us for glorious lather and sud
of ivory or dial and squirt of pert or johnsons
attaboy scalp and grinning untroubled
by comparison or sharing gurgling and spouting
fountain prank waggling peters losing piss
chasing funk and snot and blood and shit and spunk
to drain trap and beyond *oh baptize me brothers*
in heaven of steam and lofty citrus tang
of dime store cologne cuddle and scrub me
from heel to nape from wattle to taint and behind
my ruddy scruffy jug ears buff me till i squeak
fit me with harness brushed new feathers ready
to taunt the sun

hanging

there were girls along too when I was 15
traveling in a group called young
church men from parish to parish restoring
shingles or paint jobs or gardens
hosting folk masses and potluck
where we sang about god made flesh
shared in supper of bread wine molecules
juxtaposed at st francis in orangeville the boys
hung a sheet over a clothesline
and all washed together great lathering
with other hairy-assed guys pissing
and joshing and looking for once
without dread or feeling like a copperhead
sleeping next to them delighting
in music of their breath cutting black waves
on lake michigan at midnight
in a speedboat just the rough
moon and us

closer

returning to your flat
to hear water best friend
borrowing your shower
explaining his is broken
and two of you
so close he knew
you wouldn't mind
grinning
rambunctiously
his voice bounces
through a bottle
curtain pulled halfway
crooked wattled
dick curving down
like a hook his piss
escaping in careless jet
completely at ease
with you winking
drops glisten from nose
earlobes suds adorning
wilted hair of ass cleft
what exactly
is he offering is he
brother you never had
do you believe you know
the difference
between recognition
and epiphany

is this grace or is he
unapproachable
as God how exactly
do you connect
exhale or surrender
or horseplay if you ask
to compare or climb in
got room for me bro
will it ever be
the same

Bridegroom

for Tom Byrne

We closed Blue Fever at seven,
appreciating Leo's mournful
sax, getting each other's smokes,
imparting wry wisdom for the coming
attraction. We sang a lot. Beatles
mostly. Crosby, Stills, Nash and Young.
"Asking me, say, she's so free
how can you catch the sparrow?"

Each guy bought a round. Another, another
toast to my pact with Diane. Even after
Tom rushed me to the toilet,
I maintained a steady buzz. He drove us

to his club, where we sweated and rubbed
and simmered out the poisons. Took a delicious
long soapy soak, lathering each other,
loving the downpour
of hot precipitation. We drift

and wander between
our suites at the hotel. Groomsmen
poking, jostling, farting around.
Peter, Frederick, Dan, Tim, Terry,
Tom and I. *"What's the deal with this*
tie? Have you got an extra sock?

33

Where does this handkerchief go?"
Shaving brush dropped in half glass
of Southern comfort. Combs and condoms
and stick deodorant and bandaids
and Alka-Seltzer packets left on desk.

I face Tom for review. He tugs and adjusts
and fastens. Smiles. Gets a washcloth
to dab cream from my earlobe. We stand
in a row before the altar. Seven black coats.
Seven pairs of oxfords. Gentle flowers
spill from the marble table, humming

at the center of the universe. Noise lapse.
The march begins. Everyone turns
to watch Diane approach. My hair is wet,
black, and slicked back. I am crisp.
I am washed. I am sharp, shaved
and shorn. I am ready
for my bride. Tom squeezes my hand.

3

Original Sin

I couldn't say no when Trevor turned
the storage shed into an altar
where he shifted objects and ignited
the Coleman lantern, never letting
the flame up too high. There
were French playing cards and Viceroys

at the start. After awhile we played
poker for clothes when I still
understood nothing of the world,
unable to imagine what two naked
boys could do but chuckle and fart.

He would think of stupid games
like "Report Card" or "Dad's Lesson"
or "Kept After School." Tell me
to watch Jesus, heart wrapped
in garlands of thorn and flame or Our
Blessed Virgin Mother (images

taped to the wall, looking back) while I
bent across his lap or clutched my ankles.
It was astonishing, how he summoned
the elements: melodically, spontaneously,
casting a spell. I tried
to disengage (even as blows returned

me to my bone cage) noticing details
that never caught my attention before.
Rich magnificent layers of refuse
turning our clubhouse to a kingdom
of spider nest and ghost eggs. Clusters

of slick shining hatchlings that could fill
your body in a day. Spit-paper
dwellings for wasp and hornet, shriveled
purple cadaver of what might have been
a rabbit or raccoon or possum before it lost

to teeth or time. It's too easy to say
it was not so bad. The tingle I felt
or wisdom I bring with me now
to the bed, the bar, the alley. The warm
wet dock houses of jewel-eyed
invisible witnesses. Hushed

comfort of surf. You never felt
the cold dread in your gut
when Trev showed up
ringing your doorbell, over and over,
determined to deliver
the beating you always knew
was coming.

The Sailor's Companion

after Pound

When my folks still got me buzzcuts
and capguns I would climb
the magnolia, lolling in close perfume.
You rode by on a gleaming
Schwinn, howling *Blue Suede Shoes*,
circling my tree like a coyote. We both lived
in the small town of Waxahachie. Two boys

who knew nothing of each other.
At 20 you pulled me over
and kissed me. Too shy
to reciprocate, or object, I turned my head.
Asked for the speeding ticket. You called
and called. Left a thousand messages.

At 21 my grin broke, finally, through.
I wanted your tears and mine
to mix forever and forever and forever.
Why should I look for a wife?

At 22 you enlisted. Stationed
at Camp Lejeune, northeast
of Myrtle Beach. You've been
gone half a year now. The coyotes
serenade me nightly.

Your boots dragged
when you left the backyard
a jungle of spider lily
and mallow. Too dense
for me to clear!

Early autumn leaves float
the wind. Hummingbirds back
too soon from migration
hover and mingle
at the feeders. I cannot bear

to look. I'm getting old, Sam.
If you go fishing along the shores
of Cape Fear and let me
know just where, I can hitchhike
if you want me.
All the way to Lillington.

Because they are not eight

Ronnie gave up on his folks
before he was ten, and signed on
two days after he graduated
from high school. His mother would pour
the ashy, treacly scotch
until her head swarmed

with rattles and growls and recrimination.
If she wasn't strapping Ronnie's ass
in a blind lather she was
trying to get some off him. His father,

Jerome, was gone most every night, cruising
parks, men's rooms, adult movie houses.
Mornings Ronnie would hear him
in the shower, bathroom steamier
than heaven, singing and gasping sobs

by turns. Ronnie just started talking
to me when they were shearing us
in bunches, clumps of sandy brown, black,
rusty hair splotching dingy yellow
linoleum. Heaping in drifts. Some trippy

inane shit he said made me laugh.
Though I couldn't tell you why. *My precious
mane! My masculine fortitude!*
A kind of eulogy for Samson.

I never thought of it as mine
after it was cut. And you get more.

We bunked together. Closed taverns
in port. They gave us watch duty
on deck beginning an hour
before the next day. Creaming night
waves ragged claps of voltage teasing
your mind into graceful stupor.

It was steady and soothing
and Ronnie and me
would unwind. Nothing
mattered to him I think. The way
a lost balloon meanders
and bobs, tangles and glides.

Ronnie asked me why sailors
are gobs. I said you don't know?
He cradled my neck, hooking
his lips into mine. I caught him
with a rabbit punch
and he yelped and bayed. Shaking
back to his feet with guffaws,
he kissed me again.

Blood in his mouth. I spat
in the hollow of his chest
and cried some, socking
his shoulders and arms.
I said, "It's okay for you first,"

and he got in after three fingers
and rubbed my belly
whispering, singing Sinatra

(Summer Wind) and I was
frail and genuine suddenly
under hushed symphony
of leaking light, thinking
of my grandma's riddle: *Why are*
the seven stars only seven?

I don't mind if he wakes me
for a slip trip cause I get my chance
at bat as often as I like. Ronnie can turn
cook's duty for three hundred guys
into a fucking privilege. Swabbing

toilets a jokey tango
for the deranged. Sometimes he
just climbs in my bunk
and tells me gags
till we fall asleep. I do not

ask God why He brought me
Ronnie. Prince of tickles
in a kingdom of the damaged
and ravenous. Doctor for the ruined
bounce. I heard once in church
deserving has nothing to do
with grace. And I figure it's better
not to beg the question.

Turning

He had not intended to submerge or partake but the hazy blue ocean looked better and better when sweat rolled and humidity smothered him. First toes then as the water puckered and frothed and wind bounced across the surface he forgot his gut. He began to unbutton. Glasses came off. Watch. Khakis. Rocks slick with effusive vegetation tried his balance. A buddy smiled back at him. How far could he go? Where deeper? He dipped and cool respite took him. Relieved by vast gurgle and sway, up he came. Salt stinging. Profound heat eclipsed. He rattled his head and another, easier smile moved across his face. Gliding like a boat. Ear bubbles broke, one after the other. Turning his waking life.

Afternoon nap with tulips: London, 1986

Mother wanted to spend more
time at Harrod's and I, another
opportunity to savor
steak and kidney pie. I had

my poster from The Tate.
Basked in the chance
to take a taxi by myself,
pretend I was on my own, in this town

of jaded wisdom. Glistening essence
of urbane, yet avuncular comfort. I
didn't know enough at 28 to seek
the queer haunts. But excursions
I took to Little Venice with its murky,
too silent canals and Chinatown
and the Baths with gentle fellows

who didn't mind if you needed
to look awhile, were bliss
in their way. Like sharing lamb
curry, chutney, yoghurt and mint
with mama at **The Red Fort**
or hearing Shanni Wallis
in *42nd Street* at the West End.

But that afternoon, spilling
with white, chilly sunlight,
I could wish and do
anything. Dreams became
hopes and hopes inevitable
future. I lolled in

thick gravy of pie with onion
and ale and mushroom. Noticed
a green grocer on my way back
to the International. Carefully unrolled
Hockney's *Bigger Splash*, replacing
the print hanging over my desk.

Housekeeping arrived with a vase
and I tossed wet newspaper, after
ordering vodka and tonic. I removed
my clothes, cheerfully crawling
between layers of crisp linen,

singing down an azure
channel to the sea, waking
to find my tulips broken open.
Ivory and purple like robes
of Apollo, and capered
naked in breathless frontier
of my new domain,
laughing.

Alphadog

for Nate

From the very beginning
something about Nate
really set me off, hearing him
talk with the others guys
about women. There was a shift
in their tone. It wasn't leering
or salacious, but angry like, like
a seething geyser, or subtle
poison swimming the stream
of male blood. Now I am
a guy too, and probably
not especially enlightened. But he
struck me as a dolt. I would chuckle
too, when the women found names
for him they would never speak
to his face. But who could
blame them, when Nate would target
one, with his swagger and cooly-cool
disaffection. Like he was the only one
audacious enough to bring desire
to the conversation. *You know*
you want me. He knew the value of
his stock, the dark wavy curls,
the lean raw rough appeal of his
slender nose, flush and freckle

of his strong burly jaw. I remember
him flashing his milky ass
when he and Sarah swam the cold
Adriatic, diving to give me
the full benefit. Yeah he knew
I was a queerboy. We were all
MFA students and nobody cared,
and for all the repulsion
he stoked in me, he took
it in stride. He kissed me
at the New Year's Dance without
missing a beat, and there were times
when I thought we understood
each other better, than any guy
in our own tribe. One cold
groggy Vermont morning, I lumbered
to the men's toilets and found
the stall next to him. It was
easy to recognize his pajama trousers
and I greeted him, chipper
and exhilarated, as if I could see
past the partitions dividing us,
and he, again without hesitation, cracked
wise about amenities. *Why couldn't they
find softer paper?* And the pipsqueak
cocksucker poet, always
on the verge of sobs or eruption
could settle in with him, laughing
in agreement.

Cusp

Billy woke me in that cold
blue grainy hour when night is
still evaporating and morning
barely catching on. I was naked
and snapped the bare bulb next
to my bed. He was wearing
a shirt and towel at his waist.
Didn't want to leave
without saying goodbye. We
were staying at an artist colony in
Vermont, and I would slide
new poems under his door. While he
showed me primitive scrawls
of paintings, I'm ashamed to say
were lost on me at the time. I knew
he was straight and he knew
I was gay. But there was something
in the tenderness of that
moment, fraught
with possibility. Something
made me wonder, if it could be
all right. With that blinding
 incandescence in my small room,
and Billy with his wavy hair
the color of coffee beans,
skin like caramel holding me
close in that ferocious
clench. I basked in

his thick aroma. I wish now
I'd kissed him, or reached
for his towel. Instead
of taking shelter
in the canny, immediate
instant of infinite care
and let the rest go.

ghost father

for djd

he was channeling my dead
father jim though half my age sharp
and ragged black hair formidable
glasses skin like milk

from a star cluster he was one
of those canny males stifling
the impulse to snap you
like brittle kindling pugnacious

keen never looking beyond
literal substance of a word
or a glance or a hand fluttering
and flittering for connection

i fell far and fast ridiculous
bottle rocket spouting
payload for glimpse
of illumination only to end

a husk in tall summer grass
i carried sticky
history he could neither
identify nor honor
for one cold season

after another misconstruing
token or portent or signal
using a compass from another
galaxy or perhaps mine was the one

with floating dizzy needle
spinning past comprehension
the emails he never answered yet each
new residency he seemed different

the anger that drew me less toxic
and clarified i remember
waving to him across campus
gleaning lapse in understanding
greeting mistaken

for resignation as if loneliness
i yearned to shatter
only spread a cultivated virus
 the last semester we spoke
on a terrace snow scattering

delicate nets woven from icy breath
and tears but he was there
for my lecture and reading
first in line to embrace
tell me how proud he was

though i never said knowing
he was listening broke me open
deep purple zinnia spilling

rage and regret i never told

him sex is easy to forfeit
like poison you can no longer
trace i cannot bear to look
at the last and only snap

we took together or sop
the grief endlessly pouring
when i divulged to myself
the unsecret secret that he
was now and finally gone

4

Hatchling

I did not understand the rush
of grief swimming
through as I waited with mother
and saw the boy, no older
than eight, wearing light
blue pajamas with rockets
and prop planes and socks
on hobbly-wobbly legs
as he waited with his father
on the bench. His eyes could barely
open, squinting from sunlight
or anesthesia. He curled as if still
floating the amniotic sac,
knees and elbows huddled, frail
as a newborn heron peering
with useless eyes. His dad hovering
and vigilant. Mother told me
to stop in the way she does,
when helpless to forestall
my tears. Perhaps the boy was
weak or groggy only
from medication. His father
lifted him, tucking arms under
shoulders and knees of a son weightless
as origami, pieta flowering
as he carried the boy. I did not
understand the drops
that fell and fell or why

in that moment I pled with God
to save the dwindling
boy and his dad,
and of course,
me.

Eulogy

God took my father twenty-five years ago.
But not soon enough. You could say it was
somehow tragic. Even my mother
will tell you he was brilliant, talented, tortured.
Keen as a tomahawk, poised
as a rattlesnake, inspired
by cruel gods who feed on pain

and degradation. *The Luckys* he started
smoking at twelve had reached critical mass:
virility cultivated early by ritual, poison,
incantation, and endurance. "I want another
double, you worthless sack of shit. Nicky.
See this scar? Got it during hell week in '37.

Where's my fuckin' drink?" I remember him
winking (when I was maybe ten) to explain
Edith Piaf had been a nympho, and that
was my dad in a single take. Refined enough
to admire the great French Chanteuse, but
too jaundiced for true appreciation. "Talented?
I guess. But she's still gotta have that cock."

The hospital room he departed
was, of course, too white. Sunrays washed
over scrubbed and polished
surfaces: bouncing, increasing. Over-exposure
hurting the cornea. From his bed

he said he was proud of me.
You might say it's cynical to think
this was his only move. After a lifetime
of grunting and pawing. Challenging
my manhood. After whipping me
like he was striking back
at a world with no use for him.

He was finally making some pathetic
attempt to honor a bond
he could hardly stomach
since before I could piss
standing up. And what can a man
say about his father anyway?

Accidental usher into this pit
of the ridiculous? Why grieve love
that never happened, as if
speculation could heal any moment
sunk beyond recovery. I cannot tell
you how many times

I've wondered if I shouldn't
have made an effort. Easy enough
to ask now, without risk
of confronting the actual
man who was my dad, or my culpability
in this collision of conflicting need
and perception. Easy enough to tell you

I'm sorry he's gone when in truth there's no
comfort in summoning him. When it feels
so much better to pretend I never knew
him. Nothing. Nothing in this world
was good enough. If it had some shot
at splendor or grace he was there

to let you know it was just a grubby sham.
He might have devoured my sisters
and me, if mother hadn't tricked him
into gulping hot stones
from the cradle. Here and now

I mourn my father's passing. Jim
the Prick has left, spreading misery
and spite like pestilence in some other
unfortunate realm. Could a crater contain
my sorrow? Could a spoon?

Sparks and Jets

After lunch Sam got a treat, popcorn
glazed with caramel, in a box
with the words, SPARKS AND JETS.
He could think of places
he'd seen it left,

wet tunnels, bleacher shadows, freak tents
with their chipped egg tempera
portraits of hermaphrodites
and dwarfs and boys
with fish scales.

Sam said, *I want Sparks and Jets.*
The cashier had a silver crew
and always a gauze patch taped
to his left ear. Sam remembered

blue boxes of gauze patches
from his parent's bedroom
the day they would not let him
come up. When they finally did,
they were both quiet and he
could see the strange

boxes that said STERILE
and were blue and white
with red crosses. Sam could
taste the layer of cold cream

his mother applied
when he kissed her. Daddy
said he should go.
He gave Sam ten dollars.

Sam noticed the neighbor's cat
was losing hair in patches.
Radiation, pal? The cat
was called Pagliacci,
Sam guessed because of his
nightly arias. He heard

Pagliacci's outcries, his warnings
to intruders, his suggestions
to the ladies, his concessions
to anxiety and regret
and Sam would rise and join
him sitting in the bedroom
window. It was like talking to God.

That Day

He came home with a coloring book
handing it to me
without a word. His face slack
with resignation and fatigue.
Shirt damp with blotches
of sweat. He was somehow
more present than I can recall
before or since. Mother, sensing
my confusion, explained,
"The dentist pulled Daddy's
teeth to make room for dentures.
He can't talk. He can't have dinner
with us." How could a boy
so small grasp the gravity
of this event, suddenly
taking the burden
of sacrament? The distance
in my mother's voice. The solitude
as my dad removed coat and tie,
settling into his chair. Unfolding
the evening paper. How could
a simple mistake? Unfortunate
choice of words? Knock
the revolving and chaotic
globe from its axis? How
could two sentient mammals
drift so far from one another
and beyond repair? I can only

tell you I remember a flood
of sadness for a father I do not
think I liked. The profound lack
of understanding, of why
he made the trip to the grocery
store to buy me a gift. On a day
that must have been
so miserable for him.
I cannot believe it
has taken me so, so many
years to stumble upon this
epiphany. I cannot believe
I'm telling you I love him.

Manifestation

I am the immediate fact and instance
of myself as a man, apparent
or essential, reed and reed
music (trembling from gift
of wind) somber or rhapsodic,
net effect of pendulous genitalia,
hood of peter, pleated shaft, testicle bells,
blossom of father gift, usher gift,
y to x, son being transmission
of lover, luck of Cupid's draw, swing
of hammer. I am the step
again, again, of surname, on ladder
woven by my father, Jim, and his before
him, and his before, and his
before him. Where was I before
I was and where will I be
when I'm not? I am the male
cut into air, arm reaching
through space around me, everywhere
I step. Furry leg pounding the earth
in despair, in rancor, kicking up
for pairing times, reaping times, nuptial
times, leaving times. I am male choice
and must choose from acts
of men before me, acting
as I act, sum of my actions
in the equation of males who've come
and will follow after, caught in cage

of expectation from males and others
who are not. I am the male dripping
seed, mixing spit mixing sweat mixing
hurt and succor through blow jobs and hand jobs
and from behind and up against and kisses
and caresses and licks and friction. I am
the man sharing shower space
with other guys, lathering pissing singing
jostling lapsing gas in boisterous chorus
of ducks and lions and operatic tenors
and baritones. I am the man who
must know who must know
the texture of his spirit, the ripples
of his impact, dropped in the river
we trouble, scuffling somewhere
between seraphim and our last father
first father father before father. I am
the man who yearns his way back
to himself and actual wings, pulls
other men close to taste and see
who I am as it comes back
in recognition, reflection, mocks rhythm
of breeding. I am the man who gasps
and sobs and guffaws and counts off
the moments in smoke ends, songs
and jokes. I am the man who lets go.

5

Green Valiant

Where was I when God was dreaming
on the train to Kansas, crooners of the 40's
begging, filling his skull? Where was I
as he drove his green Valiant
from tent to tent to receive the blind
and indigent the feverish and the diseased?
Where was I when he was waiting
happily for anyone to share his gondola
on the Ferris wheel, moon only
beginning to slip from the branches
of maples? Where was I when his cologne
suffused the back seat, when he found
the bars all the sailors knew? Where
was I when he dragged ragged
as a kite on a dead cold Saturday
morning in late winter or floated
like a cinder among the brick
and dry steam of Harlem?
Where was I when God skated
molecules of water, vibration
too slow for anyone else
to detect? Where was I when God read
until the sun slept and hauled itself
up again, too spent and cranky to greet
the day properly? Where was
I when God was tossing down bourbon,
choking on oily tonic of old coffee, listening
to Benny Goodman, painting the trees

and mountains of Tuscany? Where was I
when God was bathing, closing his eyes
steeping in scalding bliss, lighting
a cigarette and settling back? Where was I
was I when God was shouting or singing
or weeping or praying to himself
or punching himself in the teeth?
Where was I when God was helpless
or ridiculous? When sleep left him
behind for days until he passed out
even in daylight? Where was I
when God was slender and virile and angry
and irresistible, when everything came
into focus the instant my mother's
hand touched his waist? Where was I
when God left, his light still reaching
me years after like starglow?
Waves from his radio sailing
years of empty space, sifting
into my bones.

Luck

When God was a boy
every season had its taste
and His fingers and palms
caressed the world's marvels
with arrogance and bliss: sticky

root and the spider's lush coat,
the water's brief memory
and rapture in a jackdaw's
abandoned nest. He slept in

hyacinth clusters or cool sand
or dry prairie grass that tickled
His ears and spoke to Him
all the night. The rain
had quit nine days when He

found a shuddering
brook and joined the water
as the elbow joins a sleeve.
When He stood to break

its composure the air
was a great song flowering
and unflowering the bagpipe
of His lungs. He traced

the current till a Crush
bottle shard opened
a new mouth
at the bottom of His foot. He
didn't notice till His pause
to feed and piss, then sat

and stroked the new autumn
quarter moon, wincing
at the warm bristle and chill.
Carefully He removed
the token from His sole,

placed it on His tongue,
shutting His eyes to seal
the memory. It still hangs
from His key chain. When He
kneaded the clay
to shape us, He remembered

how the talisman unlocked
the channel of His
private ocean: the edge
that brought Him to the start
of gravity, to sleep without

assuaging, and used it
to carve our eye slits,
splitting them
like husks in the Spring.

Not me

Maybe I'm on I-30 headed for home, or waiting
my turn at Tom Thumb with rice
and *Cokes* and *Fig Newtons*. Maybe I'm next
at the dentist and something comes
on the radio. Something stupid. Okay?

It's not *Handel's Messiah* or some choir
with a lofty message about salvation
and redemption. And I'm not some fucking rube.
I live in town, with the traffic and phony light
and cement. And I've heard them all
dozens of times, since before I could walk.

Just like everybody else. So maybe I'm
leafing through *Time* or *USA Today* wondering
how I'm gonna pay my water bill
this month, and I hear some lame crap
about shepherds or mystics chasing
down an oracle, or this kid sleeping

in a feeding trough. Like I'm sure
a baby's gonna care. Yeah. I know.
The "irony" of a savior starting
out in a barn. Whatever. But somehow
the words are seeping into one ear,

cause I'm distracted, as I said: and a line
drops to the bottom of the black

ocean. You see? I can't explain it.
I have no gift to bring. In that moment,
I see this blizzard of pitch
and muck and shit we crawl

through every day, everybody just shoving
and biting and beating on each other.
Nobody able to find enough time
or room to just be decent
to someone. Anyone. All you hear

is how they can't fucking stand you.
Because your car died at rush hour,
or your kid is crying, or you need
a bag of macaroni that isn't broken.
You're just something else wrong
in their lives. Another kind of torment.

Then I think of God, tearing
open this curtain. This crushing,
massive curtain of hurt
and detachment and rage. This world,
this world, this world that smacks

you and chews you to pieces
all the fucking time and God
pushing through like some greased up
maniac crossing the English channel

or silver catfish gliding
the stewy swamp, just to make sure

we know we're not forgotten
and I'm thinking. *Why?*
What difference does it make? I'm nothing

special. I'm just another guy.
Another prick. It's too late. You can't
do this. Not for me. Not me.
And yeah. Then I just break,
just break, just break.
Completely down.

Reprieve

They dispense anesthesia here
freely. By gulp, inspiration
or sting. Amnesia for damage
to marrow and nerve. Pulse
and resolution. Potent shot
of clear, pure distillation
scathing all the way down
till the world regains its luster,

and you are wiped out. Savvy blues
and rap ooze from clubs. Resigned
and enraged as a dowager
to time and disappointment. Torture
of memory and goodbyes
that were never quite enough.
I wonder sometimes if mutilation

jewelry, black lipstick, nail polish,
elaborate tattoos of predatory fallen gods
and crucified leather dolls, make it
somehow easier to bear. If piercing
the tongue with silver electrifies
a blow job or prolonged soul kiss.

I think of how God scatters us
away, far, far from reconciliation
and mercy. Flailing in quagmire
of apathy and retaliation. Ignorance.

Sailing headlong into deepening
waves of nightfall. God's orphans
shivering in the undertow
of November. Then, suddenly

snow. Drifting patiently
to gleaming crystalline
heaps. Coating everything
in a veil of blamelessness.

Flawless star flakes
aloft on airstream, tickling
nose, ear and lash, delicately
covering the head with astonishing,
weightless benediction.

6

memory more dreadful than god

consider them side by side

one swallows the other

in a moment

and you in the next

Tinman

Ah, the melancholy song
of the smithy who wrought
my inception. Pounding
rivets at my shoulders and ankles.
Gently buffing cheek and belly
to a splendid gloss. Awe and elation
mingling like a supple mother,
sudsing her ingenuous parcel
of whoops and shrieks. His touch

refined and meticulous, drumming
each layer to fanciful proportions.
He saw in me what our waking
dream of life might be, careful
to tilt my funnel cap.
Fixing my jaw in perpetual glee.

In some same way as the clockmaker
nudges toothy steel and copper jogs
to steady tempo, so did my radiant
ticking begin. Sometimes I would help
him split trunks into kindling, scoop
pockets in the earth to make a bed
for turnips or squash. Other times

intricate flakes of late solstice
would tickle the gray air and we would
join hands, springing

and cavorting. Happenstance
provides if we are only
vigilant enough to hear

the cues. Smart enough to resist
caution. Father warned me
from cloud bursts and thunder claps.
And though they were not scalding
salt drops I'd no doubt souls that left
our realm were grieving their loss

or the loss of others. I was bringing down
a maple when a deluge caught me
before I could make it home. Motion slowed
to suspension for uncountable days,
until a small girl with braids
and a man of straw anointed my afflictions.

They were on a pilgrimage to solicit
favor from a high priest of sorcery.
Sovereign in a glistening green city.
The girl and her familiar
wished only to return to the farm
where her quilt and sock dolls

waited. The straw man sought a brain
as the dull-witted are sacrificed
to petty appetites. I wanted to manage
and sort the cluster of moods I could
not name or harness. A congenial lion

joined us, hoping to recover
valiance. Man of tin, man of straw,
glorious beast, air nymph and consort.
We assassinated a crone
who could work rough-magic
in exchange for the wizard's help.

When I came back to our cottage,
my father was gone. I could not say
where. I await him still. At dusk
there is only the teakettle, owl cry
and my furious thumping heart.

what i cannot show you

there are two men

        in the photograph

if not the same they are

        close voices

dropped in pitch scales

        of manhood try fugues

and nocturnes

        on their bobbing throats

there are two men

        in the photograph

        maybe it appears

in a magazine   newspaper   facebook   instagram

                                                            twitter

            or on a website

perhaps it stretches

                    seamlessly

                              on a billboard you pass

                                                            on your way

            home from work

streams from your television

                    perhaps it dozes

                              in a shoebox

there are two men

in the photograph they share

an attachment you can guess
                    the nature but you might

                                        be wrong
        there are all kinds
of attachment and all kinds

                of men they do not touch

                                        but that is only

a clue if they know

            theyre being watched

and maybe this is

                the moment   just before   i cannot show

                                        you what

they might do

when the sun recedes   when liquor

                                              makes their blood
              tick

moment   by gorgeous   moment

                              down

                                              to the last
              follicle tip

hen they take an extra second

                         to learn

the other as they change

                    for a swim in the glimmering

eventide of late july

there are two men

                in the photograph we do not

know

what they want maybe to try

          everything theyve never done

maybe just another green

                    and geeky

hoptoad to jostle

        when insufficiency

swallows like locusts

                maybe a

taproot to spring

i cannot show you

the skittish   glee of two men
                                    no longer afraid
to merge in the salty nook

                              of trust and discovery tingle

                                                      of wishes
            revered no longer afraid

                                    of the flocks that despise

                                                      their own
            unthinkable

            cravings you might say

its he great queer lie what any two men

                                    might create given
            opportunity

                        and privilege of irrevocable

gender glorious prickle
                        of whisker against whisker lips

brushing testicle sac

                  crevasse sweet leakage

mingling

Sleep clinic

I drive past on my first visit,
doubling back to find the unmarked
building. Sprawling. Cut glass windows.
Beyond any stillness I've known.
James answers the door after I
press a button that makes no sound.

He wears blue scrubs. Interior adobe
swathed in posh earth tones of latte
coffee and dark red clay. Paintings
are blotchy, thick rectangles,
contemporary and nebulous, soothing
and non-assertive. There is no tick

or whir or hum of another. If I were
in my own nest I would wear nothing
at all, but tonight it is loose
shorts and prayers murmured
to witnesses I will never see. I watch

a disc explaining reason and purpose
behind my visit. Specialists will
meticulously track inhalation, tempo
of heart chambers as they empty
and fill. I get two glasses of ice
water and begin trawling

for the lake of infinite hush. *Lost Highway*
is unwinding on A&E and an hour
slips before James returns. He moved
to Dallas from scrubby East Texas

hills and ties his hair in a ponytail.
I remove my shirt and sit on the edge
of the bed. He applies blue gel,
sometimes rubbing it in his palms
like lubricious sap. I do not mind

when he mentions his mother's success
with gastric surgery. It's like we're
the only two there. I consider touch
between men, empty
of fear or expectation. When there's nothing

to deny or prove. Soon wires adhere
to temples and ribs, sternum and spine.
Despite sinister appearance, the headgear
with scoop and Velcro straps nestles
comfortably in place, delivering constant

current of delectable crisp, capacious,
restorative air, only for me.
It is like a game of exchanging
wordless song with Dionysus
or Raphael. This insistent gift

I must learn to surrender
and release, greedily gobbling

flavorless milk of ecstasy,

till every cell is engulfed.
Hours pass I think before James
stirs me for shift of position,
heaping and adjusting pillows. I am on
my side and returned to my drifting
boat of repose. It is a little after 5 AM,

when he rouses me, before driving
streets that might belong to a planet
without other human company.
There is only damp blackness
and yellow street lamp angels
and the radio and nothing
nothing nothing else.

Quandary

A man wakes to the sound of rain. He does not know if it is day or
night. Slips feetinto slippers. Streets empty. Out of smokes. For
some reason every store is closed. He returns to his flat. He begins
to wander and spots overflowing ashtrays. Sifting through a drawer,
among batteries and chewing gum and razors and bandages and stamps
he finds rolling papers. Wrapped in light blue with the silhouette of
a bugler. Gathering the ashtrays at the kitchen table, inspecting each
end, he arranges them in rows, calculating a new smoke salvaged from
every four cigarette ends. He has forty-three to work from. From the
radio Peggy Lee says something about the circus and disappointment.
He sets to work. Bathes before finding his way back to bed, dragging
luxuriously. Savoring the kick. *I will not sleep empty,* he thinks. But after
the new cigarettes are used up – how many more can he make from
those? And from those.

Texas Summer

You would think after more
than half a century, the washed-out
empty sky, grass mashed
down in yellow patches, wouldn't
discourage me. The neighbor cats
lolling on the sidewalk long after
sundown wouldn't invite me
to stretch out in vapid comfort
of unmeasured sleep. The broken
down drive-in movies with ghosts
of circus paintings and screens vast
and immaculate as a cotton sail,
offering nothing but silent, untroubled
absence of color or motion.
Clunky metal box speakers
hang from black poles. Skeletons
from a time when it took nothing
to find pleasure anywhere
you went, just some ingenuity
and spirit of revelry. Now mercury soars
like fever bearing down, blowing circuits,
soaking sleeves and collars and boxers
and socks. Ruining gardens, annihilating
even simple industry of brewing
a pot of cool, dark blackberry tea.
Why bother when you can surrender
to the stolid, hypnotic dance
of newspapers dragging

in rough wind, the hum
of cicadas playing voiceless
dirges, the sparkless flint
of dry wood and road kill bone,
tinder of aimless rage?

One very cold, dry perfect martini

for Peter Verrando

I remember the drink from our father's
age. By the time I reached six I knew
how the husband ended his daily labors.
Invoked his rest, the door
to dreamland in a frosty, conical glass.
World of our fathers, Pete.

Though I knew this was not a nightly ritual
in my own home, I watched enough television
to know, this is what they would choose,
if they could. Dick Van Dyke, Danny Thomas,
Carl Betz, *Honey, I'm Home*, and don't forget
Hugh Hefner and **Playboy after Dark**.

This was the conjugal bell, the daddy call,
we all recognize. Mama brushed her hair,
pinched on earrings. *Darling.* He tastes
her, briefly, with éclat. She hands him
the canny, delicate vessel
with it's one green eye, cool
and neat and potent and unspoken
and urbane.

This is your express ticket, your life
begins again with this drink.
And there is jazz and caresses

and subdued smiles. The last time

your folks visited from New York,
you showed your dad the bottle
of Gordon's and the grin
opened his face
like a quiet firecracker. If my heart

were to clamber towards
some counterfeit of gratitude,
Peter, it would be those times
we shared the small, dissolute hours
after evening had cast off,
and before the sun crept. We are
punchy and fevered and conversation

carries us far from the dock
of ordinary lives. We never tire
of the other's dreamy
soliloquy. The hand extended
to coax and fish the salty portal,

to let the squalling pipsqueak
gorge his tiny roiling bellows.
Here is Mecca. We are dressed in sharp
black jackets and trousers, our ties

show the crimp of confident fingers.
It isn't strong, but our cologne
mars the air like a shark's fin.
The summer wind feathers our scalps.

We find a restaurant where Moroccan
stew bends our senses. Potatoes
are comets, yellow onions long, soft,
sweet caresses. The pianist unlocking

delicate, wistful Satie from his keys.
Everywhere there is quiet luster
of buffed marble and brass
in a muted amber veil. The waiter

brings our drinks. Glacial gin,
the murmured longing
of vermouth, and a shock
of lemon peel. I raise the cup
without a handle, and sip
from the well where I have
swallowed and swallowed
and never drowned.

This is for you, Peter,
who found me
when this life soured
like milk forgotten
or unwanted, and made me

one very cold, dry perfect
martini, that broke my skull
wide open, that set the earth
spinning like a bright
green top.

Signal

The man across the street sits
on the stoop in front of his home.

He is smoking. You have tossed
your digs like a jittery detective.

Crawling and peering
in forgotten and inaccessible

corners, frantic bug skittering
behind the bed, under carpets,

lifting cushions, toppling chairs, scattering
contents of drawers and cabinets

to the floor in heaps. Sifting
through safety pins, stale mints, bottle

caps, train tokens, expired *Trojan*s,
for an unstruck match. Lost lighter

with residual ignition enough
to get you started. The man

across the street sits on the stoop
in front of his home. He wears

a blue flannel jacket and like you
he is late for bed. You can see

the end of his cigarette, exceeding
like a beacon with every soothing

inhalation. Unable to tell if he senses
your need, the momentary lack

you must confide or else
spend the balance of the night

searching. Where do you find
the courage to ask? It's not easy

to determine the measure
of this transaction. The *no*

that could be contempt or suspicion
or simple impoverishment.

The congenial *yes* that might be
an invitation. The man

across the street sits on the stoop
in front of his home.

For this one moment he extends
his paw offering comfort

of spark and votive

illumination. For this one moment

you are brothers of opportunity,
of contingency, of charity.

For this one moment
your connection is enough

to take the two of you
anywhere.

Acknowledgments

Poems included in *Gusher* also appeared in: *Ganymede Poets: One, ArliJo, Off the Rocks, Assaracus, Texas Observer, The James White Review, Illya's Honey, Collective Brightness, Polari Jornal, Velvet Mafia, Poetry Super Highway, Gents, Bad Boys and Barbarians, Windy City Times, Best Texas Writing 2.*

Author Bio

Christopher Stephen Soden received his MFA in Poetry from Vermont College of Fine Arts in January of 2005. He teaches craft, theory, genre and literature. He writes poetry, plays, literary, film and theatre critique for sharpcritic.com and EdgeDallas. Christopher's poetry collection, *Closer* was released by Rebel Satori Press on June 14th, 2011. He received a Full Fellowship to Lambda Literary's Retreat for Emerging LGBT Voices in August 2010. His performance piece: Queer Anarchy received *The Dallas Voice's Award for Best Stage Performance*. *Water* and *A Christmas Wish* were staged at *Bishop Arts* and *Radio Flyer* and *Every Day is Christmas. In Heaven.* at *Nouveau 47.* Other honors include: Distinguished Poets of Dallas, Poetry Society of America's Poetry in Motion Series, Founding Member, President and President Emeritus of The Dallas Poets Community. His work has appeared in: *Rattle, The Cortland Review, 1111, Peculiar, Briar's Lit, Typishly, F(r)iction, G & L Review, Chelsea Station, Glitterwolf, Collective Brightness, A Face to Meet the Faces, Resilience, Ganymede Poets: One, Gay City 2, The Café Review, The Texas Observer, Sentence, Borderlands, Off the Rocks, The James White Review, The New Writer, Velvet Mafia, Poetry Super Highway, Gertrude, Touch of Eros, Gents, Bad Boys and Barbarians, Windy City Times, ArLiJo, Best Texas Writing 2.*

www.ingramcontent.com/pod-product-compliance
Lightning Source LLC
LaVergne TN
LVHW091225080426
835509LV00009B/1166